Walrus Joins In

Simon Puttock

Illustrated by Julian Mosedale

OXFORD
UN

1

What will Walrus do?

Everyone at the North Pole was very excited. There was going to be a show and ANYONE could be in it.

'I will do skating,'
said Arctic Fox.
'I'm good at that!'

'I'll do tumbling,' said Polar Bear.
'No one tumbles quite like me!'

'I'll do singing,'
said Seal. 'Everyone
says I have a *very*
fine voice!'

4

'Then I'll do diving,' said Whale.
'I won a prize for diving at school,
you know!'

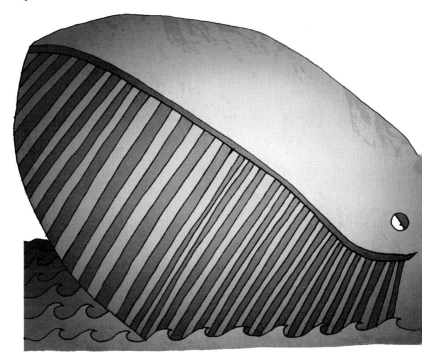

They all looked at
Walrus. 'What will
YOU do?' they asked.

But Walrus was not good at anything.

He wasn't good at skating, and he wasn't good at tumbling.

He was terrible at singing, and when he tried to dive, he always got water up his nose.

He sat and chewed his whiskers sadly.

'Never mind,' said Arctic Fox.
'You can watch us.'

Arctic Fox and Polar Bear and Seal
and Whale practised hard for the big
show.

Walrus hid behind a snowdrift and
watched, and chewed his whiskers.

He wished he was good
at something.

2

The big night

At last, the big
night arrived.
Everyone sat down
and waited for the show to begin.
Walrus sat in the front row. He was
very excited.

Fox came onto the ice and bowed.
Everyone cheered.

Then Fox began to skate. Fox skated forwards and backwards and sideways. She skated in perfect circles and figures of eight. She was elegant and amazing!

Walrus watched and he loved what he saw. Fox made it all look so easy.

Walrus was sure that if he really tried he could skate just like Fox.

He couldn't stop himself. He just had to leap onto the ice and join in with Fox. 'I *can* skate,' he cried. 'Look at me!'

But Walrus *couldn't* skate at all.
He could only trip up and fall over.

He bumped into Fox, and Fox went
flat on her face. FLOMP!

Fox was very upset. 'Walrus has
RUINED my act,' she wailed.

Next, it was Polar Bear's turn.
He rolled out across the ice like a big,
white snowball. Everyone clapped
wildly.

Then Polar Bear began to tumble. He
did jumps and spins and somersaults,
and stood on his head.

Walrus watched and he loved what
he saw. Polar Bear made it all look
such fun. Walrus was sure that this
time, if he *really* tried, he could tumble
just like Polar Bear.

13

All of a sudden, Walrus just couldn't stop himself, and he leaped onto the ice.

'I can tumble too,' he cried. 'Look at me!'

But Walrus couldn't tumble at all. He could only trip up and fall over. He tripped up Polar Bear, who came down with a WALLOP!

Of course, Polar Bear was pretty angry. 'Walrus has RUINED my act,' he wailed.

3

From bad to worse

It was Seal's turn next. She gave Walrus a don't-you-dare stare, and then she started to sing:

'*O, how my heart rejoices when I see the Northern Lights.*

My ear is filled with voices sweetly singing in the night!'

Walrus listened. What a beautiful song! Surely if he *really* tried, he could sing as beautifully as Seal? Oh dear. Walrus just couldn't stop himself *again*.

'I know that song,' he cried. 'I can sing it too!'

He leaped up and started singing along with Seal.

But Walrus *couldn't* sing! He sounded terrible. In fact, he sounded like a rusty old bucket.

Seal stopped singing and burst into floods of tears.

'Walrus has RUINED my song,' she wailed.

Whale was last. He was pretty
certain that Walrus could not ruin
his act.

Whale leaped high out of the water.
Then he fell back with an enormous
splash!

Walrus watched. He wished that he could dive like that. His flippers began to twitch, and his whiskers bristled with excitement. He tried and tried his *very best* not to join in.

But then he had a brilliant idea.

'I'll hold my nose when I dive,'
he thought. 'Then the water won't go
up it!'

Walrus just couldn't stop himself.
He *had* to join in.

'Everybody, look at me!' he cried,
as he leaped into the water. 'I can
dive too!'

But just at that moment, Whale was
getting ready to spout a big jet
of water.
WHOOSH!

Whale spouted Walrus high into
the air!

Everyone was watching Walrus now.
They weren't watching Whale at all.
They clapped and cheered as Walrus
landed back in the sea with a SPLOSH.

Whale was furious. 'You are a meddling, incompetent BUFFOON!' he roared. 'You have RUINED my act. Now GET OUT OF MY SIGHT!'

Whale was pretty scary when he was angry. Walrus turned tail and fled. He hid behind a snowdrift, feeling sad and very sorry.

4

The show will go on!

The show was over. Fox and Polar Bear and Seal and Whale stood in a line, blushing and wishing that Walrus had not ruined everything.

But everyone was cheering like mad.

'Well done, Polar Bear, well done,
Seal! Well done, Fox and Whale!' they
shouted. 'But where's the clown?
Why isn't *he* here? Where's Walrus?'

Behind his snowdrift,
Walrus heard the cheers.
Were they really cheering
for him, too?
    Yes! They were!

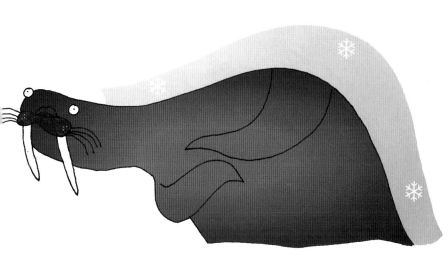

He shuffled up to Fox and Polar Bear
and Seal and Whale.
    'I'm very sorry,' he said.

'So you should be,' said Fox.

'At least everyone thought you were part of the show,' said Polar Bear.

'I suppose,' said Seal, 'if Walrus was *really* part of our next show, it couldn't be any worse.'

Walrus was overjoyed. 'Me?' he cried.
'Truly? *Can* I be part of the show? Can I
join in next time?'

'Yes,' said Whale. 'It will be a lot
safer that way. You can be the clown.
As long as you do it properly.'

Walrus practised hard and became a very good clown indeed. Now he is *so* good that Fox, Polar Bear, Seal and Whale are glad he is taking part.

Sometimes, when Walrus is clowning around, they really just can't stop themselves. They have to join in too!

About the author

I wrote this story because
Walrus leaped into my mind
one day and, no matter how
hard I tried to get rid of him,
he would not leave. He
stayed there until he had a
whole story to himself.

I don't think that I am like Walrus at all,
but perhaps my friends would say that I am.
At least a bit!